Apes and Other Primates

eye view

by Brenda Clarke

WATERBIRD BOOKS

Columbus, Ohio

 **Children's Publishing**

This edition published in the United States of America in 2003 by
Waterbird Books
an imprint of McGraw-Hill Children's Publishing,
a Division of The McGraw-Hill Companies
8787 Orion Place
Columbus, Ohio 43240-4027

www.MHkids.com

Library of Congress Cataloging-in-Publication Data is on file with the publisher.

First published in Great Britain in 2003 by ticktock Media Ltd.,
Unit 2 Orchard Business Centre, North Farm Road, Tunbridge Wells, Kent TN3 3XF.
Text and illustrations © 2003 ticktock Entertainment Ltd.

we would like to thank:
Lorna Cowan, Dr. Alison Cronin, Monkey World and Elizabeth Wiggans.
Illustrations by Simon Clare Creative Workshop.

Picture Credits:
Alamy images (18, 20-21, 22-23, 28), Corbis (OFC, 1, 5, 6-7, 8-9, 10-11, 12-13, 14-15, 17, 19, 26-27, 28-29, 30-31, OBC), Natural Science Photos (16 (J. Hobday), 24 (C.Dani – I.Jeske – Milano), 25 (Pete Oxford)).

Every effort has been made to trace the copyright holders, and we apologize in advance for any unintentional omissions.
We would be pleased to insert the appropriate acknowledgements in any subsequent edition of this publication.

All rights reserved. Except as permitted under the United States Copyright Act, no part of this publication may be reproduced or distributed in any form or by any means, or stored in a database retrieval system, without prior written permission from the publisher.

Printed in Hong Kong.

1-57768-563-6

1 2 3 4 5 6 7 8 9 10 TTM 09 08 07 06 05 04 03

Contents

INTRODUCTION 4

GORILLAS 8

CHIMPANZEES 10

ORANGUTANS 14

GIBBONS 16

BABOONS 18

JAPANESE MACAQUES 20

GOLDEN LION TAMARINS 22

RING-TAILED LEMURS 24

MANDRILLS 28

GLOSSARY 30

INDEX 31

All words appearing in the text in bold, **like this**, are explained in the glossary.

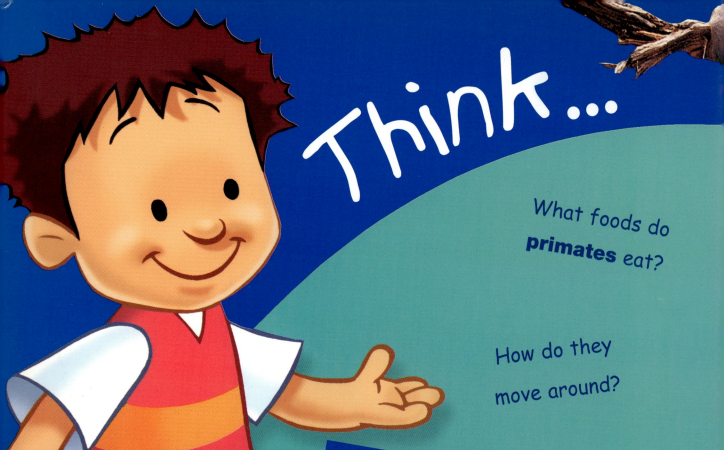

Think...

What foods do **primates** eat?

How do they move around?

What noises do they make?

How do they take care of their babies?

Apes and **monkeys** are our nearest animal relatives. We belong to a group of **mammals** called **primates**.

Imagine...

How does it feel to swing through the trees?

It looks like you are about to find out...

Hang on!

Is this a huge cave?

No! It's a gorilla.

Gorillas come from Africa. They are the biggest of all the apes. Male gorillas are much bigger and stronger than human beings. Gorillas look fierce but are very peaceful animals.

Goodnight, everybody!

Every night, each gorilla builds a sleeping nest from branches and leaves.

Gorillas have individual noseprints, like you have fingerprints!

Gorillas live in family groups. They spend their days on the ground searching for leaves and fruit to eat.

Each gorilla family is led by a big male. It is called a *silverback* because of the silver-gray hair that grows on its back. It protects the family from other silverbacks, people, and animals by beating its chest and roaring.

Carry me, mom!

A big male gorilla can weigh 400 pounds.

The only real enemies that gorillas have are human beings. Gorillas are **endangered** animals.

Newborn gorillas weigh only about six pounds. Mothers carry their babies around until they are three months old.

This is a chimpanzee.

Chimpanzees come from Africa. Scientists think they are our closest animal relative. They live in groups of up to 50 animals. A chimp is as big as a woman. They weigh 130 pounds and are about 5 feet tall. Sometimes they stand up on two legs, but mostly chimps walk on all fours.

They have hair all over their bodies and bald faces with hairy chins.

Scientists think chimpanzees make faces to show they are feeling angry, happy, or frightened.

Baby chimpanzees need their mothers to do everything for them, just like human babies. Chimpanzee mothers cuddle their babies, too!

Chimpanzees use bunches of leaves as sponges to soak up water from streams for drinking.

Can I have a hug?

Chimpanzees use sticks as **tools**. They poke the sticks into **termite** mounds (nests), then pull them out and lick up any termites clinging to the end.

Chimp hands look a little like ours.

Am I in a jungle?

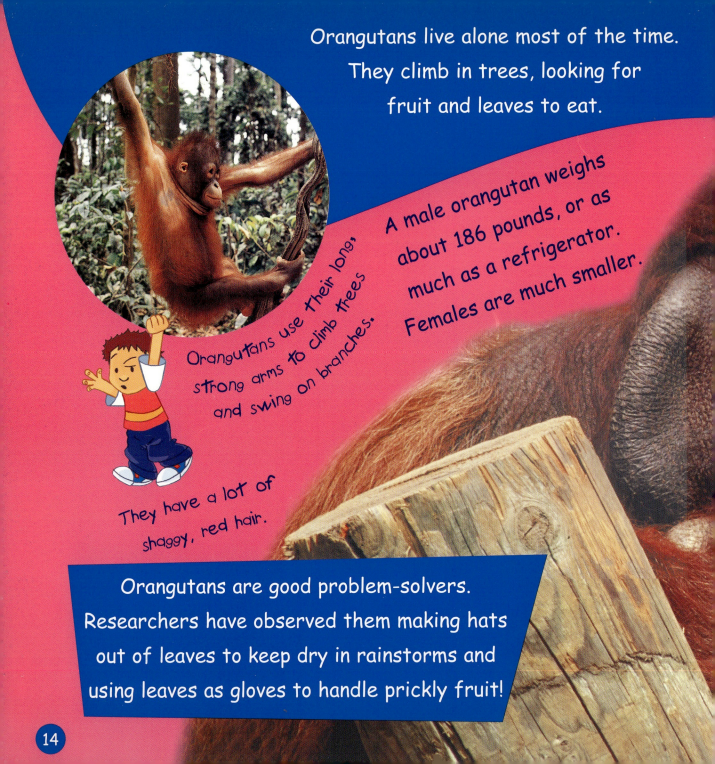

Orangutans live alone most of the time. They climb in trees, looking for fruit and leaves to eat.

A male orangutan weighs about 186 pounds, or as much as a refrigerator. Females are much smaller.

Orangutans use their long, strong arms to climb trees and swing on branches.

They have a lot of shaggy, red hair.

Orangutans are good problem-solvers. Researchers have observed them making hats out of leaves to keep dry in rainstorms and using leaves as gloves to handle prickly fruit!

This is a gibbon.

Gibbons live in southeast Asia. With their very long arms, they are the acrobats of the forest. A gibbon can leap 30 feet (about the length of a school bus) from one branch to another. They can race through the trees at 35 miles per hour.

Gibbons are usually seen stretching their long arms.

Gibbons usually stay in the trees. When they come down to the ground, they run upright, holding their arms in the air.

Hanging around is what gibbons do best.

Gibbons eat fruit, leaves, flowers, and seeds.

No! It's a hairy orangutan.

Orangutans live in **tropical** forests on the islands of Borneo and Sumatra in southeast Asia. They once lived all over this part of the world, but now they are endangered . The name orangutan means *man of the woods*.

Adult male orangutans develop huge cheek pads. Scientists believe these show females that the male is **mature**, strong, and successful.

Male orangutans make a "burping" noise by pushing air from their cheeks out through their mouths.

This is a baboon.

This big monkey is a baboon. As many as 150 baboons may live in a group called a troop. Strong male baboons guard the troop, barking when danger is near.

Baboon babies get a ride on mom's back.

Hang on tight!

Baboons live on the ground. They run on all fours.

The baboon has a dog-like muzzle.

These nice, even teeth can give a nasty nip!

A baboon has pouches in its cheeks for carrying food. Baboons eat almost anything, including birds' eggs, fruit, grass seeds, leaves, and roots. They will also eat **crops** from farms.

Sometimes gibbons catch insects and small animals for food. This is the white-handed gibbon.

Gibbons can pick up things with their feet as well as with their hands.

Gibbon families sing a sort of song together over and over again. It warns other gibbons to stay away from their **territory**. Their hoot-like calls can be heard over two miles away.

There are five types of baboons. This is a hamadryas baboon.

Perched high on a rock, this baboon looks out for enemies. Baboons don't retreat easily and stand their ground against leopards.

A big male baboon weighs about 88 pounds, or as much as a child.

These are Japanese macaques.

Most monkeys live in warm places, like Africa, India, or South America. These Japanese macaque monkeys live in Japan, where it is cold in the winter. They need their thick fur to keep warm.

Japanese macaques eat fruit, seeds, leaves, tree buds and bark, plant shoots, flowers, and sometimes crabs and grasshoppers.

Japanese macaques have red faces with no hair.

All monkeys live in family groups.

Brrr! I wish I had a warm, furry coat.

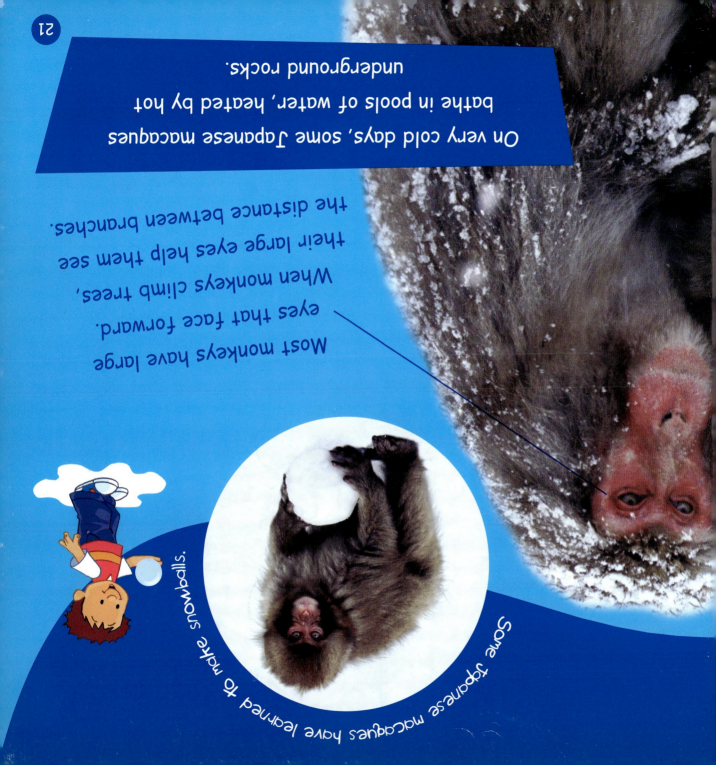

On very cold days, some Japanese macaques bathe in pools of water, heated by hot underground rocks.

Most monkeys have large eyes that face forward. When monkeys climb trees, their large eyes help them see the distance between branches.

Some Japanese macaques have learned to make snowballs.

Golden lion tamarins eat insects and fruit. They also chew holes in trees and lick the sticky **sap,** which oozes out.

The tamarin has claws, not fingernails, like other monkeys.

Golden lion tamarins can get suntans on their faces!

This lion isn't very scary.

The long hair around the tamarin's face looks a bit like a lion's mane. That is how it got its name.

This is a golden lion tamarin.

Tamarins are small **monkeys** from South America. They are endangered. The forests where they live are being cut down to make room for farms. Some zoo tamarins have been placed in **protected** parts of the forest to help build up the population.

You can tell this tamarin is a South American monkey because its nostrils point sideways. African and Asian monkeys have nostrils that point downward.

Since being protected, the number of tamarins that live in the forest has grown to about 1,000. Twenty years ago there were less than 600!

23

These are lemurs.

Millions of years ago, lemurs lived all over the world. Now they are found only in zoos or in the wild on the island of Madagascar. The ring-tailed lemur is the size of a cat and has a long, striped tail that gives it its name.

They spend most of their time on the ground, looking for food. They eat fruit, leaves, birds' eggs, and small animals.

Baby lemurs ride on their mothers' backs until they are seven months old.

Lemurs could become endangered because people have cut down the forests where they live.

Held up high, this tail could be a useful flag.

Follow me, gang!

Lemurs are not monkeys or apes. They are **prosimians**. Their main **sense** is smell (like dogs), not sight, like apes and monkeys.

A lemur has a wet nose like a dog.

Babies never lose their grip, even when their mothers are leaping around in the trees.

Lemurs have "stink fights." They wipe a smelly **scent** from special places on their wrists onto their tails. Then they wave the stinky tail at their opponent.

25

By day, mandrill families prowl around on the ground looking for food. They eat fruit, seeds, eggs, and small animals.

Looking gorgeous!

It is believed that a colorful face shows the male mandrill is strong and successful, making it very handsome to females!

The mandrill has long, sharp teeth.

Mandrills climb trees to sleep in at night.

A mandrill has a stubby tail, short legs, and a purple bottom!

No! It's a mandrill.

Mandrills live in the forests of Africa. They are the biggest of all the monkeys.

Each mandrill family **defends** its food supply. They chase away any other mandrill group that comes into their territory.

Male mandrills have blue cheeks, small beards, and red noses. Mandrills are powerful animals. They look fierce, but they usually avoid people.

GLOSSARY

APES Primate animals with no tails and big brains. Gorillas, orangutans, chimpanzees, gibbons, and human beings are all apes.

CROPS Food plants grown by farmers.

DEFENDS When an animal looks after its family and territory by fighting or scaring away other animals.

ENDANGERED When there are not many of an animal left, and the remaining animals are in danger of being hunted by human beings or of losing their habitat (the place where they live).

MAMMALS Animals with warm blood that produce milk for their young

MATURE Fully grown.

MONKEYS Primate animals. Many types have tails.

PRIMATES An animal group that includes monkeys, apes, and prosimians.

PROSIMIANS The animals that evolved (changed over a very long time) into modern monkeys. Ring-tailed lemurs are prosimians.

PROTECTED Safe places where it is against the law to hunt the animals or cut down trees.

SAP Sticky juice inside trees and other plants.

SCENT A special smell left by an animal.

SENSE Most people and animals have five senses: sight, smell, hearing, touch, and taste.

TERMITES Insects that live in huge colonies (groups). They build mountain-shaped nests.

TERRITORY The area which one animal defends against other animals to keep its food supply and family safe.

TOOLS Objects used by people and sometimes animals to help them do a particular job.

TROPICAL Places where it is hot and very rainy.

INDEX

AFRICA 8, 10, 20, 29
ARMS 14, 16
ASIA 15, 16
BABIES 9, 11, 18, 24, 25
BABOONS 18, 19
BORNEO 15
CHIMPANZEES 10, 11
CLAWS 22
CLIMBING 14, 21, 28
DEFENSE 29
ENDANGERED ANIMALS 9, 15, 23
EYES 21
FACES 10, 20, 21, 22, 28
FAMILIES 8, 9, 17, 20, 28, 29
FEET 17
FINGERNAILS 22

FOOD 17, 18, 20, 24, 28, 29
FUR 20
GIBBONS 16, 17
GOLDEN LION TAMARINS 22, 23
GORILLAS 8, 9
GROUPS 8, 10, 18, 20, 29
HAIR 9, 10, 14, 20, 22
HANDS 11, 17
JAPANESE MACAQUES 20, 21
MACAQUES 20, 21
MADAGASCAR 24
MANDRILLS 28, 29
NOISES 15
NOSES 8, 25, 29
NOSTRILS 23

ORANGUTANS 14, 15
PROBLEM-SOLVING 14
PROSIMIANS 25
RING-TAILED LEMURS 24, 25
SCENTS 25
SILVERBACK 9
SKILLS 11, 14, 17, 21
SLEEP 8, 28
SOUTH AMERICA 20, 23
SUMATRA 15
TAILS 24, 25, 28
TEETH 18, 28
TERRITORY 17, 29
TOOLS 11
WALKING 10
WEIGHT 9, 10, 14, 19

31